A Visit to My Homeland

HAITI

Yanick Louis-Lindquist

SOAR
Publishing, LLC.

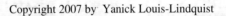

Photography by Fritz Maurice
Map by Vanessa Adam of Book Design-Book Illustrations
Designed by Terry Croom
Edited by Shannan Smith

ISBN number 978-0-9721142-6-4
Library of Congress Control Number: 2007927726

Print Executors : Citicap Channels Ltd., New Delhi, INDIA
www.citibazaar.com / connect@citibazaar.com

First Edition

SOAR Publishing, LLC
Columbia, SC
www.soarpublishingllc.com

*T*his book is dedicated

to my dear sons

Lance, Lex, and Lyle

who are my source

of inspiration for

writing the book

and keeping our

Haitian history alive.

Thank you to Elaine Rucker Smith for your help in publishing this book,

and to Monica Mills for your creative ideas, to Johanna Benitez for

editing the Spanish version of this book, and to Claire D'Ange Morel

for editing the French version of this book.

Finally, I thank my wonderful mom Marianne for giving me the gift

of life and to my family who is always there for me.

TABLE OF CONTENTS

Historical Monuments

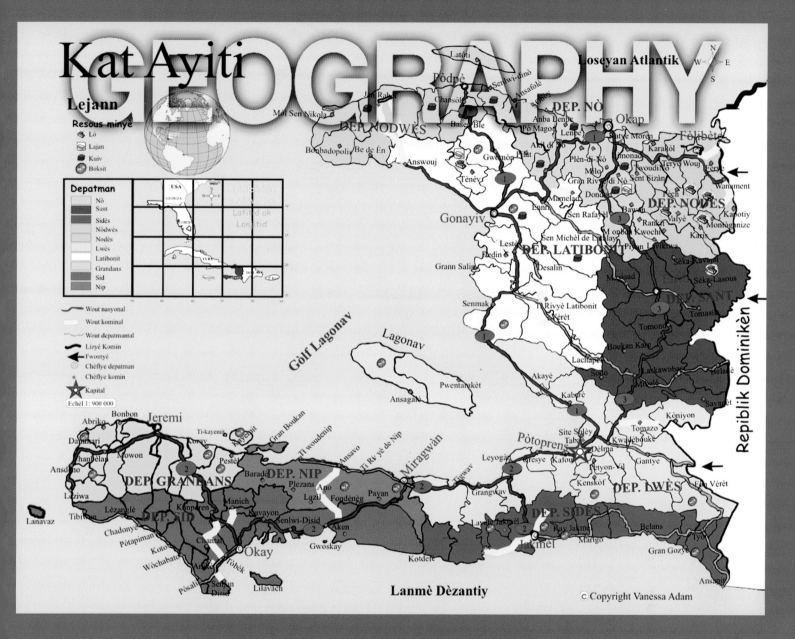

Kat Ayiti

Lejann

Resous minyè
- Lò
- Lajan
- Kuiv
- Boksit

Depatman
- Nò
- Sant
- Sidès
- Nòdwès
- Nodès
- Lwès
- Latibonit
- Grandans
- Sid
- Nip

- Wout nasyonal
- Wout kominal
- Wout depatmantal
- Lizyè Komin
- Fwontyè
- Chéflye depatman
- Chéflye komin
- Kapital

Echèl 1: 900 000

Haiti is located on the island of Hispaniola in the West Indies between Cuba and Puerto Rico. It occupies the western third of the island. The Dominican Republic occupies the eastern two-thirds of the island.

The name Haiti is an Indian word given by the Taino Arawak, a native people originally from South America who were the first inhabitants of the island.

© Copyright Vanessa Adam

1

CAPITAL CITY

The capital city is
called Port-au-Prince.
It is a very crowded place.
There are approximately
3 million people living
in the city. Hoping for a
better life and opportunity,
many people send their
children to Port-au-Prince
to live with relatives or
friends in order to
attend school.

TEMPERATURE

Haiti is a tropical island. This means that it is hot all year long. The average temperature is 79°F (26°C) with highs around 95°F (35°C). July is one of the hottest months on the island. However in the mountains, the temperature can drop as low as 50°F (10C).

ECONOMY

Haiti is considered the poorest country in the Western hemisphere. Haiti suffers from an ecological disaster. For many years, people have cut down trees to use as furewood or charcoal to cook food.

Charcoal is the only source of home energy. Since the late 1980s, approximately 80% of Haiti's energy comes from that souce. In the mid 1980s, an estimated 14,000 acres of good soil was lost each year because of continuing erosion.

4

LANGUAGE

People in Haiti speak Creole. Haitian Creole is spoken as a first language by most Haitians.
The people who have a formal education speak both French and Creole. If a Haitian has not
had any formal education, it is probable that he or she will know little or no French.

Most children are in school by the age of four years old. Unlike most countries, they do not have to stay in school until a certain age. Many are forced to leave school to help take care of the family. Children in Haiti must wear uniforms to school. The Haitian system has used standard French for many years as its medium of instruction. Since most Haitians speak Haitian Creole as a first language, the language of the school has always been different from the language of the home. Now many of the public and private schools have started to teach literacy in Haitian Creole.

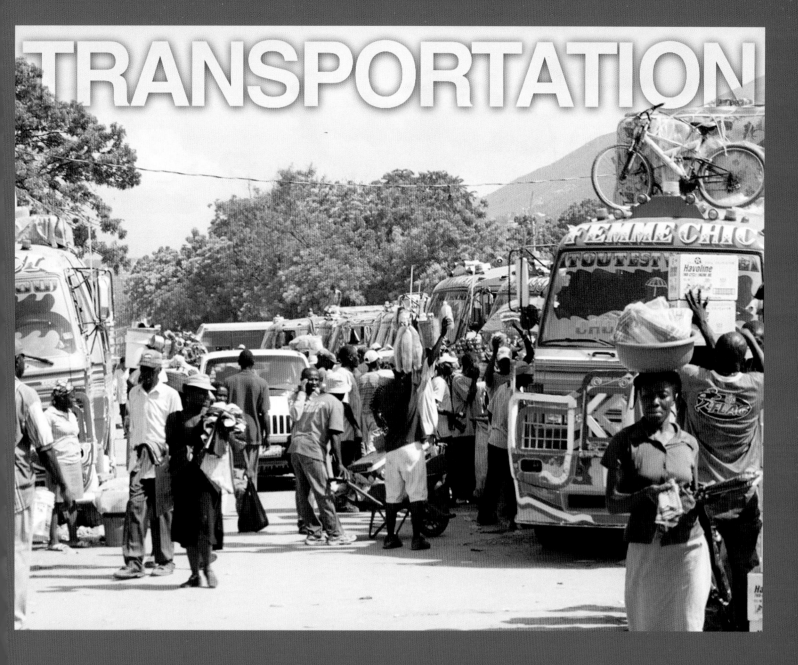

All over the city, one can find multicolored buses called "Tap Tap". The hustle and bustle of everyday life is enough to make one's head spin on a weekday morning in the capital city of Port-au-Prince. Tap Tap buses are the cheapest and the most popular means of transportation.

SOCCER

Soccer is the country's most popular sport. People are passionate about the sport.
Most young people who are very skilled are able to travel outside of Haiti, and play
competitive soccer with other players from all over the world.

THE ARTS

Haitian art is known as naïf or traditional art.

It is depicted by its bright colors.

One of the most famous Haitian artists is

Hector Hyppolite. His work is known

in many parts of the world.

These paintings are from a local artist, Franklin George.

His work is very typical of Hatian art.

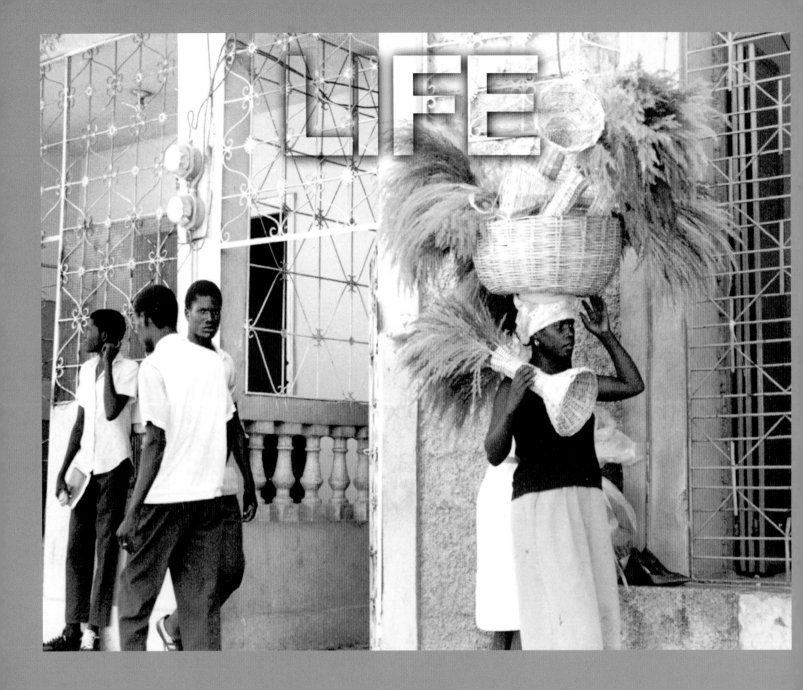

Life in Haiti is very hard for most people. Most parents work extremely hard to send their children to school. They hope that their children will find a good job and make enough money to get the family out of poverty.

Most street vendors carry their baskets of food on their head. Many walk very long distances to sell their goods.

Haitian Food is very tasty. The traditional dish on New Year's day, which is also Independence Day, is pumpkin soup. This soup is filled with a variety of fresh vegetables such as cabbage, turnips, and carrots and beef.

A typical Haitian dish is fried pork called griot, which rice and beans and fried plaintains. Rice with dried mushrooms called djon djon, is a favorite dish which is served on special occasions.

Many vendors also sell their products at the open market. The food is usually fresh from the farm. People like to bargain to get the best price for their merchandise.

BEACH HOME

This is a sample of a beautiful home located on the outskirts of the city.

These luxurious homes usually belong to wealthy families.

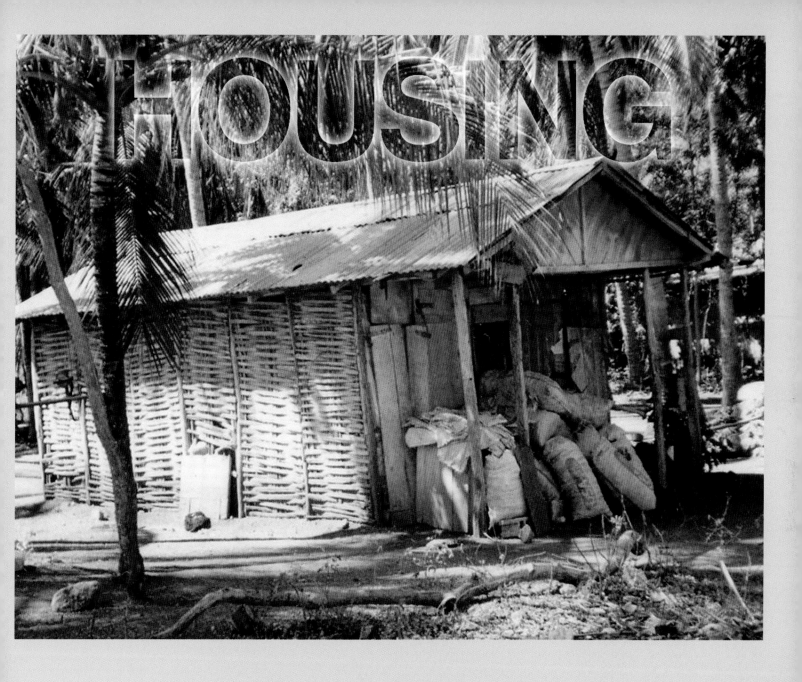

HOUSING

This is a typical home in the countryside made of straw with a tin roof.

It is often shared by at least two families.

These multicolored wooden carriages are known as "bourrette". They are usually filled with crushed ice mixed with a variety of syrups.

This delicious refreshment is called "Fresco".

People love to sip on one to quench their thirst on a hot sunny afternoon.

18

LANDMARKS

This is an old fort called *La Citadelle La Ferriére. The Haitian people began construction on this fort in 1805 and completed it in 1820. It is situated on top of a mountain overlooking the beautiful historical town of Cap-Haitian located in the northern part of Haiti. This fort was built to protect the people from French invasion. They feared that the French might return, enslave them and take over the country. Although this did not happen, the fort remains a very significant historical symbol and a crowned achievement for the people of Haiti.*

19

PALACE OF SANS-SOUCIS

This palace was the home of King Henry Christophe,

a firm but effective leader during his reign.

It was constructed at the base of the fort, La Citadelle.

20

THE NATIONAL PALACE

This is a picture of the National Palace in Port-au-Prince. Many presidents have resided there since 1915. It was constructed during the American occupation which took place from 1915-1934 in Haiti.

THE NÉGRE MARRON

This statue made of bronze is called Négre Marron located across the National Palace in Port-au-Prince. It is of a freed slave blowing on a shell symbolizing the calling of other slaves to the struggle of freedom from the French slave owners.

HAITIAN FLAG

The Haitian Flag is blue and red. The blue represents the black population of Haiti,
And the red stands for the people of mixed races known as "mulatto".
The Haitian flag symbolizes unity among its people and pride for their independence
from the French.

FACTS TO REMEMBER

Naif : *Also known as primitive or traditional -It is the most popular art form in Haiti*

Port-au-Prince : *Capital of Haiti*

Haiti : *Means high mountain. It is the first independent black republic in the western hemisphere*

January 1 : *Haiti's Independence Day*

Language : *Haitian Creole and French*

Population : *8 million*

Currency : *Gourde*

Erosion : *Study of plants and animals in relation to each other and to their environment*

Invasion : *To go in and attack in order to conquer*

Haitian Flag : *The colors are blue and red. The color white was cut out by Jean-Jacques Dessalines, one of Haiti's revolutionary leaders after Haiti won its independence to exclude forever the symbolism of the French masters who held the Haitians in bondage*

Religion : *Christianity and Haitian Voodoo*

Haitian Voodoo : *Old religion brought by the ancestors from West Africa to Haiti*

EVERYDAY EXPRESSIONS

English	Hatian Creole
Good morning	Bonjou (bon zhew}
Good afternoon/evening	Bonswa (bon swah)
What is your name?	Ki nom ou? (kee non oo)
My name is	Mwen rélé (mway ray lay)
Where do you live?	Koté ou rété (ko tay oo ra tay)
What is your telephone number?	Ki niméwo telefòn ou? (kee new meh-ro telefon-oo
Stand up!	Kanpé! (kan-pay)
Sit down	Chita! (shee-tah)
Don't do that	Pas fè sa (pah fay sah)
Speak quietly!	Palé Dousman! (pah-lay doos mah)
Open your book!	Ouvé liv ou (ew-veh-leev-oo)

MEET THE AUTHOR

Dr. Yanick Louis-Lindquist is a native of Haiti. She was born in Port-au-Prince, the capital of Haiti. She now lives in Miami, Florida with her husband and three sons.

Dr. Louis has been a language specialist for the past 19 years for both children and adults.

Dr.Louis earned a Ph.D in Bilingual Education. She is fluent in 4 languages including French,Haitian Creole, English, and Spanish.

In her spare time, she is a volunteer traveling across the globe educating and mentoring young people. She also enjoys reading and dancing.